INSIDE OUT

Creating Work Environments that

Lead to Exceptional Customer Service

Jeff Sullivan & Jennifer Good

ISBN: 1460901703
ISBN-13: 9781460901700
Library of Congress Control Number: 2011902059

ACKNOWLEDGEMENTS

Thank you to Julia Sullivan, who provided commentary and advice throughout the writing of this book. Her editorial comments and ideas for organizing the content were extremely helpful, especially on those days we felt like quitting!

Thanks also to John and Pat Sullivan. They provided their valuable opinions and encouragement throughout the eight months it took to write this book.

We also want to thank a few friends for reviewing the first draft. Thanks to Eileen Gross, Jill Airey, Tim Eggen, and Brian Mackenzie. They provided comments that helped us to provide a sharper focus on certain points and to elaborate in areas needing more explanation.

Our thanks goes out to Laura Sita, who participated in countless debates with us on the topics covered in this book. We'd also like to thank her for creating the diagrams we've included and for her imagination which led to the design for the front cover.

Thank you to Kathleen Good for providing her comments on this book from the perspective of a college student studying business.

TABLE OF CONTENTS

INTRODUCTION

This book is written for anybody who hires or manages Employees. It explains how to create a work environment that will naturally lead to outstanding Customer service. What you create on the inside will be experienced by Customers on the outside. When done well, top-notch Customer service grows naturally. It isn't easy to do, but, as we'll describe, it has been done well at some of the best and most successful companies. We'll tell you how it's done, and we'll explain why it's worth the effort.

We've recently experienced an era of recession, poor sales, and flat growth in our economy; and many leaders wonder how they can possibly keep Employees motivated and Customers happy. The strategies described in this book can help you reduce turnover, improve performance, leverage peer pressure—the most powerful form of supervision—to motivate Employees to meet or exceed expectations, and cultivate an enthusiastic culture that makes Employees go that extra mile, enjoy coming to work, and tap into their full potential. Customers can feel this culture, and it will ultimately create your organization's reputation. Competitive markets richly reward companies that know how to put the right Employees in the right jobs with the right strategic values and training. But markets are unforgiving of companies whose people practices ignore these principles.

The style of this book is unconventional, but we think you'll like it. Each chapter addresses an important aspect of building a work environment that leads to great Customer service. At the beginning of each chapter, Jeff addresses the principle anecdotally, drawing upon his twenty-five years of experience in human resources roles for successful companies such as Southwest Airlines, Office Depot, JetBlue, Jenny Craig, Fender Music, Elizabeth Arden, Cranium Games, and others. He also talks candidly about some of his less successful (but highly entertaining) endeavors. At the end of each chapter, Jennifer provides commentary on Jeff's stories, drawing on her own 25 years of experience as a communications and human resources expert in the public, nonprofit, and private sectors.

The book begins with a story about how Jeff Sullivan lands his first job in the business world, cleaning bathrooms on the nightshift for Southwest Airlines. The book ends with him consulting with some of America's top CEOs and fully understanding the concept of improving Customer service from the "Inside Out." You will, too. We confess that not all of Jeff's stories have a teaching point. Some of them—well, we just thought they were funny, so we included them.

Note: Throughout this book we have purposefully capitalized Employee and Customer to emphasize their central importance in the business world.

CHAPTER ONE

IF THE PERSON DOESN'T FIT THE JOB, IT'S TIME FOR CHANGE

Jeff's Story

Until 1983, I was the lead singer in a rock-and-roll band, playing at clubs throughout the Southwest. I had recruited my brother and all of my best friends into the band with promises of fame and fortune. We had purchased an old green van and "fixed it up" by stapling some used shag carpet to the interior. We then purchased a row of junkyard airline seats, bolted them to the floor, rented a U-Haul to carry our sound equipment, and went on the road. My teenage sister really wanted to come along, but my parents made it very clear to me that this would not happen. I quickly understood why. Traveling with a rock-and-roll band—partying in a new club every night—turned out to be a lot less glamorous than I had imagined.

One morning in 1983, I woke up in a cheap hotel room somewhere in New Mexico. The night before hadn't gone well at all. I had experienced this eye-opening moment—this "how did I get here and how do I get out" moment—as we finished our last set in a rundown club. The club had a sign that said "no guns allowed," but the sign was nearly unreadable due to all of the bullet holes. The club was filthy, and the characters who hung out there were, well, let's just say they were less than desirable people to have in your life. The back door led to the desert, which also served as the men's room.

When things like that start seeming normal, something is terribly wrong. I remember thinking that I had been on the road for one hundred days straight and too many of the clubs resembled this one. If one more critter asked me to play "Free Bird," I thought I'd lose my mind.

We were good, had a great following, and loved our music. Yet something was missing. There was no order in my life. I would be gone for two months or more at a time without ever setting foot in my own home. Every day was different: strange people, strange places, strange places to sleep. My job was to make hundreds of different people like me each night yet I couldn't take the time to get to know any of them. I built no solid relationships. I'm sociable, I like people, I like figuring people out, and this life of chaos was just not fitting what I valued. My job was no longer the right fit for me.

I could have just ignored the unsettled feeling I was having and kept doing what I was doing. Many people choose to do that. Doing nothing seemed like the easiest choice at the time, but it wasn't what I wanted. I sat down on the stage at the end of the night and looked around. Something had to change. I needed something more predictable.

I was hoping that when I awoke the next morning I would feel a lot more positive about the current state of my life. Yet when I opened my eyes, gloom was still overshadowing everything I saw and everything going through my brain. I had no desire to get out of bed. What was the purpose? Absent a miracle, my current trajectory seemed to be headed nowhere. Maybe the fame and fortune would come—but when? And at what cost?

That morning in New Mexico, I decided to break up the band. It was a heart-wrenching decision. It felt a lot like failure—quitting my dream and letting down the band members I had sold on the original scheme. But in retrospect, I think that breaking up the band was the bravest thing I had ever done. My family and friends had made tremendous sacrifices so that I could live my dream, but the lifestyle just didn't suit me at all. It was time for me to move on. And hardest of all—it was time to tell the other band members to do the same.

Once out of bed and showered, I decided to go collect my last paycheck as a future rock star. I had played at this particular club many times and knew where the owner lived. He answered his door wearing a bathrobe and immediately started giving me a hard time about whether he would pay me or not. This was normal behavior for him, but I found it particularly irritating that morning. We bantered back and forth as usual, and eventually he went into his house to get my money. As I waited outside, I finally could feel a glimpse of hope. The hope came from my realization that I would never have to do this again. The thought of being handed a paycheck every two weeks, with no drama involved, seemed really appealing.

The club owner returned carrying a large cigar box and opened the top. On one side of the box was my money, and on the other side was a .38 revolver. I think he was joking, although I'll never be completely sure. But for some reason, it immediately struck me that it represented the turning point I was at. The .38 represented staying on the same miserable path I was on. The money represented doing something better.

This guy, not one of my favorite people in the world, seemed to be enjoying his little game. He said, "I'm not sure which one I should take out." Have you ever noticed that miserable people just love making other people miserable? Obviously, I did get the money, rather than a bullet, because I'm here twenty-seven years later writing a book. I tucked the money in my pocket and walked away thinking, *What now?* It felt good though. I was on my way to a more predictable and stable lifestyle, assuming I could find a steady job.

Jennifer's Take

In the interest of full disclosure, let me begin by mentioning that Jeff Sullivan, the co-author of this book, is also my brother. The sister who wanted to travel with his band, well, that's me. Our writing sessions for this book included Jeff reminding me of his stories as I typed as fast as I could. We shared stories and ideas for hours and hours. I took notes of all of those business related conversations. I say "business related" because we laughed a lot, complained a lot, and talked across multiple topics each time we met for a writing session. The plan was to write a series of short books, this being the first.

So, on to my "take-away" from Jeff's rock-n-roll story. His story makes me think about two important lessons that are helpful in business as well as with personal success. First, so often people set their eyes on a certain goal, as Jeff did with becoming a superstar! They work hard towards that goal, perhaps for years. At some point they may begin to realize that they aren't happy, or they're on the wrong path. Yet letting go of that original goal becomes harder and harder. After all, they've worked so hard and so long, how can they give up now? So they continue being unhappy. They continue on the wrong path.

What I've learned is that letting go of something that isn't working is often very hard. It's as if today's misery is better than the unknown of what will happen if you let go. Yet once you do let go, you realize all of the other opportunities you've been missing. That's what Jeff did that morning that he chose to break up his band. He let go. Read on and you'll learn about the many opportunities that then came his way.

The second lesson has to do with something most people in the business world have experienced too often. That is, people who are not a good fit for the job they're in. You've probably worked with them. Perhaps you've been someone in the wrong job yourself. Jeff was in a job that didn't suit him. It would have been easy to coast along on the wrong path; instead he found the courage to find a new one. When the person doesn't fit the job, it's in everybody's best interest to make a change. Jeff was wise enough to make the change on his own.

Have you ever had Employees who emotionally quit the job but who keep coming to work? Their attitude and lack of enthusiasm infect everyone around them. But something makes them stay. Perhaps it's fear of change, or just getting used to being unhappy. Recognizing this as a manager, and taking corrective action, is a key component of creating an energized work environment. You won't get happy Customers from unhappy Employees. This is a key concept to the "Inside Out" approach.

CHAPTER TWO

MAKE YOUR EMPLOYEES
FEEL IMPORTANT

Jeff's Story

I had dropped out of college after one semester—not understanding how that sort of education could advance my career as a rock-and-roll superstar, and never imagining that the day might come when I'd need or want a Plan B. I had no experience in the corporate world. I had no permanent address, no money, and no assets. I didn't even own the green van any more—I'd sold my share to my brother. I had walked away from the life I knew—and into what? Believe me, there were days that I doubted I had done the right thing. I like knowing where I'm headed, and at this point I did not.

I had absolutely no idea what to put on my resume. I could sing and write songs and play a guitar. I also, remarkably, had a pilot's license. I love airplanes, and my father, a fighter pilot, had taught me to fly at a young age.

My search for employment soon landed me at the airport in Austin, Texas, where I was living at the time.

I managed to get a job at the private terminal, fueling airplanes on the night shift. Because I no longer had my old green van, I would ride my bike to the airport for the midnight shift. Very occasionally, I would get to fuel a commercial airplane, which for some reason was the highlight of my week. It made me think about how great it would be to work for a major airline. I love to travel, and airline Employees could fly for free! That seemed like a really good fit to me! An idea began to form.

I set out to find a job with a major airline. I filled out applications with every airline at the Austin airport, except for the newest and smallest of them all, Southwest Airlines. Southwest was an unknown back then, and I just didn't feel the pull to apply. Hardly anyone had ever heard of it, and I wanted something big!

After many interviews and many rejections, I was offered a job sitting in the airport parking lot accepting tickets. Not quite what I had planned. I worked for the airport, not for an airline, and was not going to get to fly for free. Being rejected for the other job openings was disappointing, but at the time I really just wanted steady work. The job wasn't great, but at least I didn't have to pack up a stage full of equipment every night and drive to a new city, and I was handed a paycheck every two weeks without drama. I no longer worried that I wouldn't get paid. My expectations were fairly simple. I was also close enough to the airport to track job openings on a regular basis.

After about three months at this job, a friend of mine who worked for Southwest encouraged me to apply. He told me about the people he worked with, how much fun they all had together, and convinced me that it was a great place to work. I didn't hear about people who loved their job too often, so it seemed worth a try. It certainly sounded better than sitting in a parking lot. When I finished work one afternoon, I went into the airport and filled out a Southwest Airlines job application. Then I waited.

It finally happened. About four months after breaking up the band, I got a part-time job with Southwest Airlines in Houston. I was at the bottom of the organizational chart, scrubbing bathrooms on airplanes on the night shift. It was a dirty job on the worst possible shift, but I saw it for what it was—a foot in the door with a great company. Now I had everything I had wanted on that day I decided to break up the band. I had a steady job and a steady paycheck. I had stability. I had hope that I'd be promoted into a job that would be more challenging. I felt like I was finally on my way. I was determined to stand out from the crowd and decided to be the best bathroom scrubber there was. I wanted to meet as many Southwest Employees as I could, and I wanted to learn all about the airline business. I began to volunteer for everything I could and would take on extra projects whenever possible.

Some of my fun loving coworkers realized how little I knew about the airline business and decided to play a joke on me. They told me that Herb Kelleher, the Chief Executive Officer of Southwest Airlines, was going to be flying his helicopter into the Houston Hobby airport. They sent me out to where they said he planned to land, conveniently in a spot where as many people could see me as possible, and told me to keep waving the lighted batons they had given me. I stood out there waving those batons while my coworkers got a good laugh. Herb didn't have a helicopter, and if he did, he never would have landed it in that particular spot. I took it all in good humor but realized that I had a lot to learn. Everything about working in this new world seemed completely foreign, and I guess that was obvious to everyone around me.

One thing I soon noticed in the business world was how quickly people size each other up. The pilots and flight attendants were never rude to me, but there was this subtle way everyone had of treating me as if I were a step below them. Passengers did the same. They thought the uniform I used to scrub airplanes communicated something important about who I was. We all judge far too quickly, and I have never forgotten that lesson.

I had been at Southwest for four months in December 1983. A friend of mine, Chris, who worked the same job and shift as I did, invited me to come along with him to the company Christmas party. The party was in Dallas so we would have to fly there and back in the same day. I was enjoying my free passes on the airline, but this particular trip sounded like more trouble than it was worth. I wouldn't have gone without Chris's encouragement. He kept saying ,"You're really gonna like Herb." He was referring to Herb Kelleher.

"Why?" I asked.

"Just wait."

I was a little nervous about this because I had no experience with executive types. However, I was certain that we wouldn't actually talk to Herb. Certainly he would have more important people to talk to than Chris and I.

We landed in Dallas and went to the party. It was a huge and very lively event. Southwest Airlines really knew how to throw a party! Herb was at the front door. He was, and is, imposing when you meet him. He is big, tall, and has a loud and commanding voice. He was personally greeting everyone as they came in.

As we walked in I was shocked when Herb said, "Hey, Chris!" Now, Chris had told me that he had only met Herb once before, at the previous year's Christmas party. Chris also lived in a different city from Herb so they never just ran into each other at work. So I was surprised when Herb remembered Chris's name. Herb asked Chris a few questions about Chris's art collection, which they had discussed, once, a year before. I was impressed, to say the least.

Herb then began talking to me. He was incredibly friendly and personable and didn't make me feel like I was beneath him in any way. It seemed that we were all on an equal playing field.

I later came to understand that Herb was legendary for his incredible memory. He always knew people's names and something about their personal life. Everyone at Southwest looked up to him. Everyone admired him. He made a huge impression on me that evening.

I admired and respected Herb so much that I became even more interested in doing a great job and learning all I could learn about the airline industry and Southwest. Because of his leadership, I just had this feeling that Southwest was different from all the other airlines. I was proud to work for Southwest, and I would look at the airplanes as if they were my own. The airline industry became more and more interesting to me as I began to pay attention to the business itself and follow trade publications about the industry, competition and regulation, legal battles, airplane specifications, and anything else I could find. Like most people, I learn easily when I'm really interested in the topic.

Two months after the Christmas party, after my first promotion to ramp agent, I went to the Ronald McDonald House to volunteer for an evening. Southwest had encouraged Employees to volunteer for that particular charity. I entered the Ronald McDonald house and found out that I was volunteering along with Herb. Herb saw me and remembered my name from the huge Christmas party and our short conversation. I began to realize that small things can have a big impact and began to understand the importance of taking a personal interest in the people around you. That Herb remembered our short conversation made me feel like a real person—not just a cog in a wheel. It made me want to work even harder to stand out.

We spent the evening cooking dinner, baby-sitting, reading stories to children, and cleaning up. At the end of the volunteer shift, I offered to drive Herb to the airport. Now that I had a job, I'd purchased the old green van back from my brother, and that's what I used to chauffeur Herb. I did warn him that it had no air-conditioning and the heater was stuck on. Keep in mind that this was Houston and was very warm outside. I may not have mentioned that my green van was uncomfortable and it smelled. Anyway, he didn't complain. On the way to the airport we had the usual small talk but also had a conversation about the airline going into Denver. It was a fairly small airline back then, and going into Denver would be a really big deal. I had been reading so much about what our competition was doing that I was able to hold my own in this conversation. I am sure I sounded naive to Herb as I asked questions based on articles and books I had read. But Herb wasn't the type to make anyone feel naïve so he answered all my questions and seemed really engaged in the conversation.

At the end of the ride, as I pulled up to the airport, Herb looked at me and said, "Jeff, you want my job don't you?" We both laughed and he got out of the van.

This short ride in the old green van may seem like a minor incident. Insignificant. Yet I still remember it twenty-seven years later. What a difference from my days in the band—where I'd been forced to stare at a .38 just trying to get paid! As I drove away from the airport that day I thought to myself, *Wow, I have a job, a real job.* I had my foot in the door with a great company that I knew could take me far if I was willing to work hard and do what I could to shine. I also trusted and admired the company leader, something I very quickly learned was an integral part of creating a great work environment. Because Herb cared about his team, his team cared about making the company successful.

Jennifer's Take

Every now and then, you find that great Employee who is excited for opportunity and enthusiastic about increasing his or her talents and skills. This is the type of Employee who, with experience, you can give anything to and he or she finds a way to get it done. Although Jeff's first job with Southwest Airlines was far from glamorous, he came to the company with that "can do" attitude that we all should look for when hiring for any position. Our next chapter is on hiring and we'll discuss how great companies hire great Employees.

Have you ever walked into a business and immediately been irritated with the poor Customer service you receive? I think we've all had that experience. What's amazing is that a Customer can immediately pick out poor hiring choices and can immediately recognize a lack of training. Yet managers often overlook this. Walk through your business from the Customer's perspective. You'll see things very differently.

As Jeff reminded me of his initial meetings with Herb, it made me think about the huge impact leaders can have on Employees without even realizing it. Just as it's important to walk through your business as a Customer sometimes, managers and leaders should also walk through as a front line Employee.

Herb Kelleher has and had a huge impact on his Employees because he took the time to care. He was fantastic at validating others, giving them hope, and making them feel important and appreciated. The trust and admiration that Herb built within his company led to his Employees wanting to go that extra mile and make the company successful. He cared about his team. This was a huge component of the work environment built at Southwest Airlines that led to their reputation for outstanding Customer service. Make everyone feel important.

CHAPTER THREE

HIRE FOR ATTITUDE

Jeff's Story

My big promotion to management came in 1986. I had been promoted into a flight attendant position previously, and now was being offered a position at the management level. My job, along with one other person, was to begin a systematic recruitment function for Southwest Airlines. I was going to spend my days interviewing and hiring. Truth be told, my *only* interviewing experience was that I had hired a drummer for my band. The qualifications I had defined for my drummer were that he could play the drums, had a place to practice, was willing to tolerate horrible working conditions, and didn't expect to make much money. Yet now I was involved in building a hiring system for a fast-growing airline that wanted and needed to maintain its unique brand identity. Clearly, it was not my resume that landed me in this new job. Although I had asked for the job, I was bewildered when the opportunity was finally mine. I felt like the dog that caught the car. What now?

Southwest trusted me with a very important job. I was too excited to reflect on why they had given me the opportunity. However, looking back on it, I am sure that I got the position because I was known as someone who loved my job and was willing and able to learn. I was definitely hired for my attitude rather than my resume and that lesson stuck with me. Attitude can make or break a career.

I took my new management position very seriously. We wanted the people we were hiring for Southwest Airlines to support our brand identity. We were quirky. We had an unusual group of people, we liked that, and we wanted to figure out how to keep that. I mean, who would paint a plane like a killer whale? Southwest thought it was a great idea. To keep this quirkiness, we knew it all depended on hiring the right people, and Herb was trusting me to do that. I remember one conversation with Herb about all of this. Although thankful for the opportunity, I was a bit nervous about how to handle this new challenge well. He said to me, "Jeff, if you are sitting here wondering who here knows more about any of this than you do, there isn't anyone." He was learning, too, yet was also a great coach. I've always been tuned into people—I notice their behavior, and the things that seem to motivate them—and I guess Herb had picked up on that during the time we had spent together. Herb was able to recognize abilities in people that they didn't even fully realize themselves.

Southwest was growing so fast that our brand identity easily could have begun to fade away. This happens at many businesses as they attempt to handle growth. We were hiring hundreds of people in hundreds of different ways. There were neither standardized processes nor descriptions of the types of people we wanted. I began to notice that many Dallas Cowboy cheerleaders were becoming our flight attendants. I wondered about this. I remember asking to see the written notes of one person who was responsible for hiring and seeing "nice legs" written on the application. Was this one of our qualifications? Actually, at the time, I believe it was! With no system in place, our culture could slowly change, and we all knew this would also change the Customer experience. Something had to be done!

We began by centralizing all hiring processes to our headquarters office in Dallas. We then developed the beginnings of a hiring system that would end in our goal of hiring for attitude and firing for attitude. Our best chance of hiring right was to find hungry, energetic people who had a great attitude that fit with what we were trying to do as an airline. We began to define that certain type of person who would be successful with Southwest Airlines.

As part of the hiring process, prospective Employees had to take a drug test. One day, the lab called me with good news and bad news. The good news was that my applicant's drug test came back negative. The bad news was that the applicant was a German shepherd! Some people just wouldn't fit in at Southwest!

As I interviewed people all day long, seven days per week, my goal was to put applicants in front of hiring managers who I knew stood a chance of being successful. It wasn't unusual for me to interview twenty-five people before I'd choose even one as a potential aircraft cleaner. Because I had started as an aircraft cleaner myself, I personally knew the opportunity I was offering someone who had that special spark we needed. I wouldn't pick just anyone!

We continued to refine the hiring system. *What is causing success in this job? What is causing failure?* We looked for patterns and talked to the people doing it well. What did they have in common? My first focus was on flight attendants because we were hiring so many of them at the time. We began to realize that the person most capable of picking the best flight attendant was the best flight attendant in the company. We also talked to supervisors about problem Employees and identified common behaviors related to failure. Finally, we developed a process to use in identifying the best applicants. We were willing to accept a lack of experience for an abundance of attitude and energy.

When I talk about hiring for attitude I am often questioned about the need to also hire for specific skills. Obviously there are some positions for which a baseline skill level must be required. At Southwest Airlines for example, these positions included our pilots and mechanics. But when we really thought through it, we realized that most of our frontline positions really didn't require specific skills. Success had more to do with natural talents and attitude. However, if specific skills are an absolute necessity in your organization, find your pool of applicants with those skills and then focus on the natural talents and attitude needed for success in the job and within the organization.

How do you measure attitude? When I use the word *attitude* I use it very broadly. Let me provide a specific example from the hiring system we put in place for flight attendants. Our first goal was to have a large applicant pool from which to choose. Building a reputation as a great place to work is one important key, and at Southwest we had achieved that. Our reputation was the only advertising we had to do for employment. The great work environment we had built on the inside created a great reputation for us on the outside. We guaranteed that *all* applicants meeting our minimal qualifications would receive a job interview. We found that this increased our applicant pool even more. We charged ten dollars to apply, which helped defray the cost of hiring and training people to interview. At the time, we were receiving twenty-five to thirty thousand applications per year.

We carefully trained all interviewers. We also trained some of our best flight attendants to participate in the interview process on a rotating basis. We identified specific dimensions to look for in applicants that experience had shown were directly related to success on the job. Sense of humor and empathy for others are examples. These traits fit in perfectly with the image we wanted to portray to our Customers. It had to begin with hiring right.

We traveled to major cities and conducted group interviews. Typically the interviewers consisted of one person from human resources and two flight attendants. We used many techniques to evaluate applicants in these group interviews. Sometimes we'd ask them to tell us a story or a joke, or tell us about something they'd experienced. The applicants that made this cut were then brought in for one-on-one interviews. Again we used an established list of dimensions. We did extensive studies on this and continually updated it. We designed our interview training around recognizing "the right fit" for Southwest Airlines. Applicants who made it to the one-on-one interviews were interviewed by three separate people. Each person used different techniques and types of questions. This was the process we began using for *all* job categories, not just flight attendants. At the end of the day, teams would get together to compare evaluations of applicants. The team made hiring recommendations to our hiring committee, and then final decisions were made, with attitude as a very significant decision factor. As you can see, we took hiring right very seriously.

Jennifer's Take

The pattern of "Inside Out" becomes clearer in this chapter. Southwest took great effort to hire the type of people that matched the reputation they wanted to maintain. It was so important that they designed the complex and thorough hiring system Jeff described. They knew they couldn't be known as the "fun" airline to fly if they didn't hire people who truly valued "fun." Reputation begins with who you hire.

You may be frustrated with your own hiring system yet not have the resources available to a company like Southwest Airlines. If so, here are a few tips.

Begin by sketching out the entire life cycle of your current hiring system. It begins with recruitment and ends with the Employee's first day on the job. Analyze this entire cycle and attempt to pinpoint where improvement is needed. Problems often exist at the very beginning with recruitment. Ask yourself how people become aware of you as an employer. If a job opportunity is your product, how are you marketing that to the public? Poor hiring choices so often begin right here, with how and where jobs are marketed. Are you getting the right people to apply?

Another common problem area is untrained interviewers. Hiring well is a learned skill. Interviewers must fully understand and be able to recognize the talents, skills, and attitudes they are looking for. Asking questions such as "Are you able to work under stress?" will likely get the answer of "yes" if the applicant needs a job. A better method is to ask for examples of how the applicant handled stressful situations.

As you walk through your hiring system, step by step, focus on one problem area at a time. From advertising methods to the Employee's first day on the job, there are opportunities at every step to do things well or poorly. Are interviewers trained? Do they know what they're looking for? What impression do applicants have of the workplace? Is the orientation process dull and boring, or exciting and motivating? Find as many ways as possible to be unique, effective, and memorable. It doesn't have to be complicated. Simple things like sending flowers or a gift with the final written job offer will be remembered and will bring the new Employee in with a positive attitude.

Jeff mentions that Southwest Airlines had built a reputation as a great place to work and this improved the quality and quantity of their applicant pool. This is a step in the recruitment process that is often overlooked. Your organization's reputation has a huge impact on who will apply for your job openings. To attract the best you have to be the best place to work. What you create on the inside becomes your reputation on the outside.

CHAPTER FOUR

CULTIVATE CULTURE

Jeff's Story

During the late 1980s and early 1990s, Southwest Airlines was becoming a cultural phenomenon. We had appeared on the front of *TIME* magazine, *Newsweek*, and every major television network. A couple of best-selling books were written about the airline. From 1987 through 1994 we were listed as one of the top places to work in America. Southwest Airlines became so interesting to people that we even had our own reality show for a few years! Southwest Airlines pulled the plug on it only because it got too distracting.

Herb continued to do his part to maintain our unique brand. A press conference was being held one year for the top five companies in the one hundred best companies to work for in America. Herb sent me in his place and requested that I wear the orange jumpsuit worn by our ramp agents. At first I was horrified! Was he joking? He wasn't. I attended the press conference in my orange suit next to four power-suited CEOs. If I'd still owned the old green van, I'd have driven it to the event for added impact. The orange suit made a statement about our company that was important to Herb: at Southwest Airlines, every job is important and we're all in it together, from the executive suite on down the line. It was part of our culture.

Up until this point in time, Herb had been able to somehow touch all aspects of our growing airline. He was our icon. His good humor had a major impact on the evolving culture of the company. I can remember back then when I was working long days, seven days per week. One day I was talking to a potential group of new Employees. I was telling them how we all worked hard. I explained that every time I came out of the building at eleven p.m., feeling sorry for myself, I saw the boss's car still there. As I finished this statement, Herb, who was standing beside me, leaned over and whispered, "Jeff, my car has been broken in the parking lot for three weeks." He had a knack for ensuring that people didn't take themselves too seriously.

We had grown 1,000 percent in size since I began with the airline yet had managed to not lose our unique culture. We were so focused on keeping this unique brand and holding onto that "high touch" culture that we formed a Culture Committee. The Culture Committee had rotating members and was made up of people from every level of the company. They were top-notch Employees. Their job as members of the Culture Committee was to be the unfiltered eyes and ears of the company and hold onto the "Southwest spirit." This "spirit" contributed greatly to the Customer experience we strived for and was a top priority for the company. The Culture Committee would plan activities to promote the spirit and culture of Southwest.

Any organization could adopt this Culture Committee idea. There are many ways to do it well. At Southwest the entire committee would meet quarterly. Employees would serve two-year terms on the committee. Colleen Barrett (who later became the company's president) and I were the only two permanent members, and that was only to provide ongoing leadership to the group. At our quarterly meetings we would divide up into subcommittees. Each subcommittee was assigned certain activities and projects. As an example, a subcommittee might be assigned the task of conducting a touring party. They would go to a certain city and throw an appreciation party for all the Employees based in that location. Committee members might help with party coordination, leading activities during the party, or even filling in for Employees so they could take a break and attend the party.

One of my favorite accomplishments of the Culture Committee was a book they put together and provided to all Employees. If you read the book from one side, it was filled with stories of how our Employees did extraordinary things in difficult situations. When you got to the center of the book, you'd flip it over and read from the other end. On this end, the book was filled with stories of how our Employees didn't do a great job in difficult situations. The book was very enlightening and read by everyone. It helped all Employees understand expectations.

As the airline grew, we knew that we would have to rely more and more on management to hold onto our existing unique culture and the Customer experience for which we had become famous. The company was getting too big, and it was impossible for Herb to form personal connections with each Employee as he had in the past. Whatever magic Herb had up until this point now had to be maintained in a new way.

Herb began a new requirement that every executive must work at a line level position at least one day every three months. I believe this policy had many benefits for Southwest. Even for executives like me, who had been promoted up through the organization, the velocity of business change was so great that it didn't take long to lose context of what our Employees were going through. It is critically important for management to fully understand the impact of decisions they make at a very tactical level. When you actually put on a uniform and wash airplanes or serve drinks, you are able to fully understand the impact of decisions from the executive team on Employees and Customers.

Here's an example. As we got bigger we had a harder time keeping our planes on time, and we were known as the on-time machine. This was critical to our operation. One of the reasons we were so profitable was that our planes were in the air a lot more than airplanes at other airlines. Yet the incredible growth we experienced came with operations that got more and more complex. I remember one executive who worked in the department that ran ground operations. After having worked all day on the ramp on a Saturday, and talking to the other ramp agents, he realized something so obvious. There should be a clock on the Jetway that counted down the number of minutes until the airplane should push back. The idea was implemented, and it made a big improvement to our on-time status.

I believe that in any organization, managers should take the time to do the job required of their Employees. It provides a renewed appreciation of how difficult it is to work with the public. Front-line Employees in any organization deal with a lot of stressful situations, and when you're a manager five levels up from that position, it's critical that you understand the impact of your decisions. Decisions have a domino effect, but management often only focuses on the impact of their decisions just one level below them. The line of sight you have from the decision you make to its impact on the Customer has to be clear. Requiring executives to work at the line level kept this line of sight open at all times.

To further benefit from the policy of executives working at the line level, Herb would require everyone to stand up at executive meetings and give a five-minute talk about what job they did and what they learned. They'd also be asked if there was an Employee who should be recognized. In Southwest's *Spirit Magazine*, you'd often see articles on Employee of the month, who were often recognized when officers worked in the field.

I learned at Southwest, and later in many other companies, that organizational culture happens only from carefully and methodically focusing on the details of the work environment. It takes time, persistence, and a focus on evaluating each and every way that the organization impacts its Employees. Four of the most obvious ways are through hiring practices, compensation and reward strategies, performance evaluations, and training. But there are hundreds of other touch points where Employees are influenced, from the time clock to afternoon breaks to work space to small comments from the boss. Through all of these touch points, organizational culture develops.

Little things mean a lot and contribute to building and sustaining culture. For example, at Southwest Airlines every Employee got a birthday card from Herb, hand signed. For my own staff, I would ask them what the most important day of the year was for them, and on that day I would remember them in some small way. One Employee said the most important day of the year was her mother's birthday, so I sent flowers to her mother on her mother's birthday. Many companies don't think about all the different ways to recognize and appreciate Employees, but little things matter a lot. I learned that at Southwest Airlines. I learned that Employees will care about the company if company leadership shows they care about Employees. Similarly, Customers will receive special attention if Employees receive that same attention from leaders.

Even something as insignificant as a time clock is part of the work environment and provides opportunity to have an impact. One company I later worked with used this opportunity as Employees checked in each morning to communicate to everyone. Employees would clock in and receive their daily two-minute update that included anything interesting happening within the company that day or just any message managers wanted to distribute for the day. They viewed the time clock as a moment to communicate with Employees each and every morning.

Creating the right work environment is challenging to say the least, but the great part is that once that right environment is created, desired culture happens naturally. Performance problems are reduced, and people who don't meet expectations are naturally and quickly weeded out. They just don't fit in. Peer pressure, the most powerful form of supervision, leads people toward behaviors that adhere to organizational values and goals. Money is no longer wasted by having the wrong people in the wrong jobs. Communication strategies are in place to ensure that expectations are consistently and clearly communicated. An enthusiastic culture makes people go that extra mile, enjoy coming to work, and tap into their full potential. It's worth the effort.

I have a great story from Southwest Airlines to illustrate great culture at work. In 1991, fuel prices went absolutely through the roof. Fuel represents the second highest cost for an airline—next to labor. During this time it became our highest cost —by far. It put us and other airlines in a really dangerous situation. Unlike our competition, which furloughed and fired Employees, our Employees of their own volition decided to take voluntary deductions from their paychecks. These deductions went into a fuel fund to help defray the cost imposed on us. We neither laid off nor furloughed a single Employee. What more can I say? It was a natural re-action given the culture that had been created at Southwest. We were all in it together.

Fast-forwarding a few years, in 1999, I was hired as a consultant by a group of airline executives wanting to start a new airline which eventually became JetBlue. One of our first meetings with this group of executives took place in a hotel in New York City. Working with this group of executives who began JetBlue provided me the opportunity to test what I had learned—and to see if we could create another great work environment from the ground up. Imagine my amazement as I found myself coaching these experienced CEOs on people leadership at the start of this new adventure. Me—who at one point could barely scrape together the money to buy back the old green van. This experience, which I discuss more in Chapter 8, further reinforced to me that careful and creative attention to building the work environment is the only way to reach sustainable desired culture.

I have found that you cannot effectively legislate Employee behavior with a bunch of procedures and rules. Values control behavior, and successful organi-zations must define those values, and hire, fire, train, and reward towards those values. This leads us into our next chapter.

Jennifer's Take

Creating organizational culture in a new company is far less challenging than changing culture in an existing company. Culture develops from the ground up, from the work environment, and cannot be legislated from the top. To change culture, you must first change the work environment. There are hundreds of ways Employees are impacted by the work environment, and each of these touch points contributes to the formation of culture. With desired culture in mind, take a microscopic view of your work environment and focus change efforts there rather than demanding change from the top.

An analogy may help understand the distinction between creating a work environment and attempting to impose culture. Think of it this way. Cactus grows in the desert and orchids grow in the rain forest. If I put a cactus in the rain forest, it will die. If I put an orchid in the desert it will die. The same principle applies to people and behaviors. Different people thrive in different environments. Different behaviors thrive in different environments. Decide what kind of culture you want for your organization, and then create the work environment that will make it grow.

One of the greatest challenges to expect as you work towards growing a new culture is that many Employees won't fit in. The result will be resistance to change. Existing Employees were hired to fit in with the existing culture. Many of them are quite comfortable with this culture, and aren't likely to share your motivation for change. You have to expect and plan for some resistance. Expect turnover. The gap between current culture and desired culture will determine the amount of turnover you can expect. It will happen over time as you begin to create a new work environment, focusing on each and every touch point. Eventually, the new environment will weed out the people and behaviors that no longer fit. This isn't to say that these people or those behaviors are bad; but just like the orchid and cactus analogy, they won't thrive in the new environment.

CHAPTER FIVE

INCORPORATE STRATEGIC VALUES INTO YOUR PEOPLE PRACTICES

Jeff's Story

One of the biggest lessons I learned throughout my career was that successful organizations always had an underlying set of strategic core values. I learned that having these strategic values was the foundation for all people practices and ultimately for desired organizational culture.

In our personal lives, core values drive every decision we make and everything we do. People who value good health may act on that by taking time to exercise every day. People who value humor will find reasons to laugh. People who value their time will work efficiently. You get the point.

The other thing about values is they don't change much. Values create a consistent pattern of decisions and behavior, which leads to consistent types of experiences, which usually serve to validate existing values. This circular pattern means that values are pretty rock solid whether you are super consciously aware of them or not. They become so baked in that acting against your core values just won't feel right. It will create internal conflict, both for an individual and for an organization.

Figure 1: Circular Pattern of Values

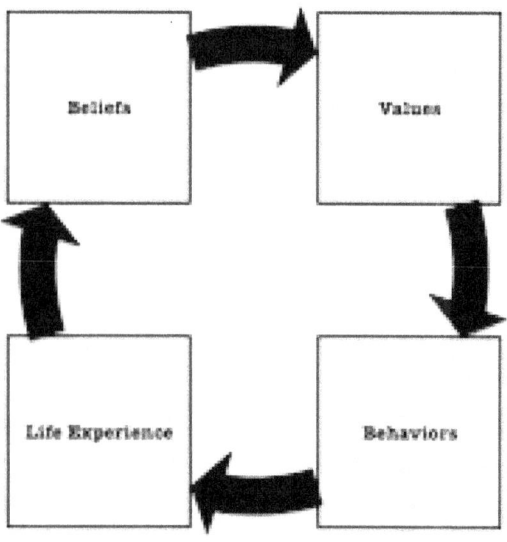

The only time you tend to see someone's core values change is when they are faced with a major and life-changing event. Examples are bankruptcy, the birth of a child, or a sudden death in the family. Life experiences such as these will serve to change future daily life experiences, which alters the circular pattern. This can sometimes lead to a value being changed.

Organizations, like people, also have a collective value system that drives behavior. During my years as a consultant, I've had clients tell me that their organization did not have values and that they wanted help creating some. Each time this happens, my answer is the same. "Yes, you do have values in this organization." You may not have formally declared those values, you may not even know what they are, and you may not even like them, but values determine behavior and all organizations have values. Those values might be serving to hold back the success of the organization or maintain the status quo, but there are values underlying every decision and action.

I have also realized that most organizations have both declared and undeclared values: those that are published and those that are silent but often even more powerful. A declared set of values that hasn't been embraced by the Employees doesn't really govern behavior and is completely useless. Your Employees will bring their own undeclared values to your organization, and your Customers will experience them. To have just one set of values in an organization, they must be integrated in all decisions and all people practices.

I once worked in the corporate headquarters of a large national hair-styling business. I was visiting one of our largest locations and heard about an Employee the manager was about to fire. This was an Employee who did a great job and who had been very dependable. She traveled to work each day by bus. There was a bus strike, and this woman was now having trouble getting to work. The manager's first reaction was to fire her. To me, this behavior was based on a value of convenience for the manager. Legitimate challenges that a great Employee was facing were just an annoyance to the manager. This went totally against declared organizational values. I scheduled an Employee meeting and together we came up with a plan to help the Employee get to work until the bus strike was over. Many Employees volunteered to help. The plan worked well, and we gained a very loyal Employee who developed a very loyal Customer base. My actions were based on the true organizational values. Declared values have *no* value if they don't impact decisions and actions.

Just as it is difficult to change culture, it is also difficult to integrate new values into an existing organization. However, with values we are talking about something very specific. Values are a part of culture. Culture is much bigger and broader. While it is difficult to integrate new values into an existing organization, I have found that if something happens to shake things up, we often could create the needed momentum. A merger, new leadership, or impending bankruptcy are examples of major events that can create this momentum. Absent a major event such as this, I have worked with leaders to create needed momentum by clearly communicating a need, urgency, or reason why change is critical. Everyone must understand the "why" before change can even begin. This is challenging, but I have seen it done well.

Here's an example of creating a triggering event that provided momentum for a very specific change effort. I worked for a popular game company as a consultant. It was a fun place to work and had a high energy and creative culture. The founder was the icon. He was playful, approachable, had a great sense of humor, and loved games and toys. His office looked like a little kid's room. The culture there was so strong that you couldn't survive unless you had a passion for playing games. It was a joy to work there. Staff meetings involved sharing ideas for new games, and then about four hours of playing new games to see if we liked them. The founder hired an executive from a competing toy company to be the new COO. They were considering taking the company public and thought that an experienced executive would provide needed credibility. Her management style had worked well at her prior company, but she seemed like a drill sergeant within the culture of this particular game company. She did not last long and eventually moved on. The culture was so strong that it weeded her out, just as I would expect. Setting a company like this onto a new course, given its strong values and strong culture, would need an important and motivating trigger to maintain momentum.

One group of Employees had been pressuring the founder to expand from just games to games and toys. The founder knew that this would be expensive and there would be a lot of risk. It would involve changes to marketing, manufacturing, and even hiring. Where do you look to hire toy makers? It would involve significant change.

The triggering event we created was a goal. The founder set a target of hitting certain financial goals with the gaming business. He told his Employees that if they could hit that mark, management would invest and expand into the toy-making business. He used a focused and specific goal that was motivating to his key Employees, and they did hit the mark. They became known and successful as both a toy and game company.

This company, like every successful organization in which I've had the opportunity to work, used declared values as the compass for all decisions and actions. I realized that this was the essence of great leadership: making decisions based on organizational values. It is a simple concept but difficult to do. Values need to control your hiring procedures, performance management, communication techniques, compensation plans, and all of those touch points that influence Employees. Defining values is only the start, but all too often it's where people stop. Defined values are etched into a plaque, hung on the wall, and forgotten. Integration makes them come to life.

It's important to once again touch on the importance of hiring people who will naturally fit within the organizational culture. I said that you should hire for attitude, and attitude comes from values. Great companies hire people based upon the organization's values. They reject those people whose personal value system would be greatly at odds with the organization's value system. It is rare but possible for an individual with differing values from the organization to eventually fall in line with organizational values. But two other scenarios are much more common and very costly for an organization. I've seen both scenarios many times. First, hiring people whose values conflict with organizational values leads to high turnover. This is costly for an organization. People either quit because they don't fit in, or they are fired. Second, and even worse than high turnover, is that people with conflicting values might stay. That is, they won't adhere to organizational values but won't quit and won't get fired, at least not for a while. They start infecting others and causing organizational stress. They spread their attitudes, and a new set of values, those undeclared values, begins to set in.

A major benefit of integrating organizational values into all people practices is that these values serve to clearly define the "right" way and the "right" results. This may seem like a simple concept, but it took years in the business world before it became crystal clear to me. The "right" way refers to those expected ways of behaving in the organization. They become part of the culture. The "right" way is the "way things are done around here" for Employees. It was interesting to me as I worked in multiple organizations how the "right way" could be so different from one organization to another. When Employees don't understand the true "right way" they often just bulldoze their way to a goal, creating chaos behind them. The "right" results are typically easier to define because results are usually somehow tied to financial outcomes and/or market share. Nevertheless, successful organizations consider their values when defining any organizational goal.

Figure 2 is the chart I use to help me understand right way and right results. There are Employees who will fall into each of these quadrants. For instance, all organizations have Employees whom everyone likes and who seem to make friends easily, but who do not achieve the right results. This is a "right way but wrong results" Employee. These four quadrants were helpful to me throughout my career as I evaluated Employees and as I evaluated organizational culture.

Figure 2: Right Way and Right Results

RIGHT

WAY

WRONG

Right Way; Wrong Results

Right Way; Right Results

Wrong Way; Wrong Results

Wrong Way; Right Results

WRONG ← → RIGHT

RESULTS

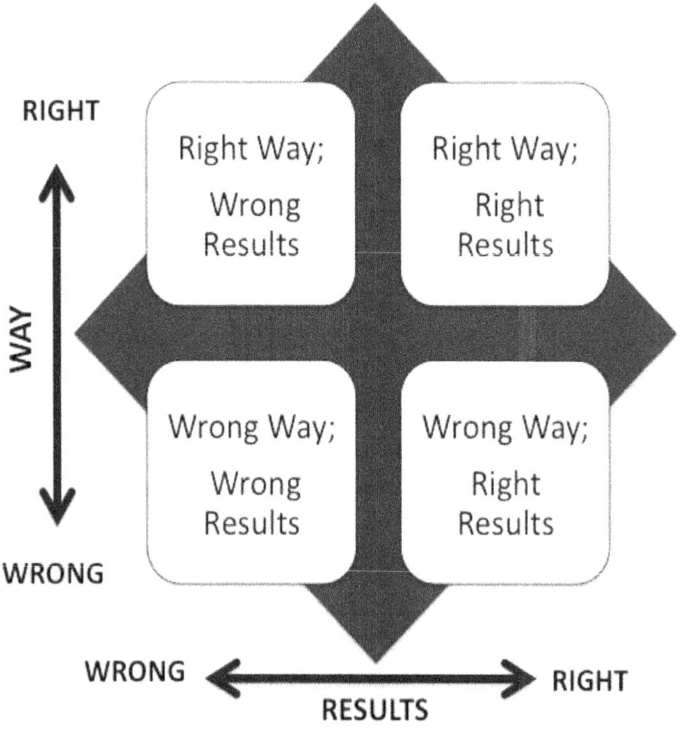

There is a perfect story about a large package delivery company and their Employee reward system that illustrates the importance of values and how those values should impact the "right way." Their leaders thought they could make more money if their drivers could increase the number of deliveries they made per day. They came up with a reward structure that encouraged making as many deliveries per day as possible. Drivers sped up, tossed packages at doorsteps, raced to the next address, and their leaders were happy for a little while. It didn't take long, however, before leadership began noticing a new trend. They were receiving more and more complaints about mistakes. The wrong packages were being delivered to the wrong addresses. They put one and one together and eventually realized that their reward system was causing mistakes. If nothing had been done about it, if they hadn't made the connection, eventually leaders would have ended up with a culture that valued speed over accuracy. In the long run, this was no cost savings at all. It actually slowed everything down and cost more. These Employees accomplished the "right results" which was delivering lots of packages, but the "right way" had not been defined. Organizational values must define and communicate both.

When values are effectively integrated into an organization's culture, great things begin to happen! Employees begin to make good decisions simply because they understand organizational values. They understand the right way. Managers no longer have to refer to a gigantic rule book for making decisions. The work environment changes, and you take one giant step forward towards growing a new and improved organizational culture.

Jennifer's Take

Too many people have been through the process of identifying ideal organizational values only to have nothing change. This experience leads to a belief that defining values is not that important for an organization. This couldn't be further from the truth. The problem is that values must be defined and then integrated into all people systems. The integration part is where too many organizations fall short.

Here's an example. One of the major people systems in any organization is the rewards and recognition program. When you reward someone, not only is it motivating for the Employee, but you are also teaching everyone else about values. *If I do what that person does, I'll get rewarded, too.* All of your rewards programs should be based on organizational values. Do you value integrity? How can you tie rewards and recognition to this value? There are so many creative ways to do this. You could have a quarterly integrity award wherein one Employee is highlighted and the story of how they displayed integrity can be communicated to everyone. Someone gets recognized, and everyone else gets a lesson about organizational values. Recognize an Employee in the company newsletter after they went through a great challenge in order to fulfill a promise to a Customer. Integrating a value into the rewards structure means to reward and recognize the behaviors that stem from those values.

Jeff explains how values help define the "right way" to do things. Let me further clarify this point. Let's say that your organization values collaboration. This word can have multiple definitions; my idea of collaboration may be completely different than yours. Jeff uses the phrase "behaviorally based values" for good reason. Once values are defined, expected behaviors to result from those values must also be specified. For example, with collaboration, a behavioral expectation might be to seek input from your team, or be open-minded to new ideas. If an organization values imagination, expected behaviors could include listening openly to all ideas and using brainstorming activities during meetings. The point is that Employees must clearly understand the right way to adhere to each organizational value.

We have all worked with people who do *what* they are asked to do but perform in a manner that ends up being destructive to the organization. For example, consider the salesperson who bad-mouths other sales team members with the goal of making all of the sales on his own. He ends up having a high sales volume, the "right results," but his methods were not the "right way." His "wrong way" methods become part of your organizational culture, which eventually impacts the Customer experience. Stress and chaos on the inside will be experienced by Customers on the outside.

Great companies all have something in common: a well-known and clearly identifiable culture that makes them different and memorable among the competition. This culture stems from their values. Southwest Airlines is known for humor and efficiency. Google and Apple are known for innovation. It is interesting that all of these organizations have a clear set of organizational values. What is your company known for? If you can find people who share common values and those values drive them to act in accordance with the strategic objectives of the company, you've got a pretty solid foundation for success. The values that guide behavior in your work environment will be the values that Customers feel on the outside.

CHAPTER SIX

TRAINING INSTEAD OF RULEBOOKS

Jeff's Story

In both my personal and my professional life, I always have believed that the real challenges in life are not the ones that you can answer by reading a rulebook—the real challenges arise when you have to make decisions based upon your sense of "what is right." The measure of a person and an organization—any organization— is their intuitive sense of "what is right." This cannot be legislated. It all comes down to values. Training is a key component of engraining the "right way" into organizational culture.

When I became part of the Southwest Airlines management team, the company had no training programs other than those required by federal safety regulations, and our human resources department existed largely to push paper. As we continued to grow, we realized that we needed a strategic human resources function to continue delivering a unique Customer experience during a period of unprecedented growth.

Many experienced managers were hired to bring their knowledge and skills to our growing company. They also brought along their policies and procedures from other airlines. We watched the volumes of policies and procedures continue to grow and become more complex. We used to refer to it as the "Big Green Monster": four large phonebook-sized volumes! Something about the Big Green Monster reminded me of the old green van, held together by rope and duct tape. I know that all organizations have to have some sort of a rule book, but the problem is that they all end up looking the same.

I think the idea of the Big Green Monster was to answer any and every question a manager might have. Managers began to rely on this rather than exercising their own judgment. Unfortunately this isn't all that uncommon in businesses, but slowly the realization came about that it wouldn't work for Southwest Airlines. We wanted managers who knew how to make the right decisions. We needed training, not manuals.

We hired for attitude, which cannot be taught, but we also needed to train to bring understanding of how things should be done at Southwest Airlines. In 1987, Herb gave me an opportunity to begin building, at the ground level, a management training program for Southwest Airlines. Herb put his trust in me, and once again it was time to figure out the best way to meet this tremendous challenge.

Our training program evolved over many years. I can't say that we had it exactly right at the beginning. Our first "training center" was an off-balance converted Jetway. If you put a ball in the center of the room, it would roll to the front. I used to joke with our Employees telling them to be careful not to fall off their chairs!

To make a long story short, this whole project turned into what became known as People University. We developed our own in-house adjunct faculty. Just as we had done with hiring, wherein the best Employees helped hire new Employees, we realized that the people who were already successful at doing something should teach others how to do it. They could say, "I've been in your shoes," rather than "I've always been in human resources." Some Employees were selected to train (it was an honor), and all executives were required to spend a certain amount of time training as well. Our senior executives learned about leadership as they taught lower level managers. They'd get challenged on *why*, and it made them think. Our teachers learned as much as the students.

Our People University continued to grow and improve. It was where much of our brainstorming took place and where new ideas were tested. By the time I left Southwest Airlines, it was a full-time job fielding requests from people around the world wanting to visit our People University. To get some control over all the requests, we began holding an open house for People University with speakers and a planned agenda for visitors. It would sell out *fast*, and every time. The price of admission was a donation to the Ronald McDonald House.

The success of People University eventually led to our ability to reduce the size of the Big Green Monster down to about a hundred pages. It contained Federal Aviation Administration and safety regulations, Equal Employment Opportunity Commission requirements, etc. We called it Guidelines for Leaders. We knew that no policy manual in the whole world could predict every situation a manager might encounter, but we could provide some basic guidelines. Our training strategy was an important key in enabling our managers to make the right decisions and reduce that Big Green Monster!

In 1994 I was offered a job with Office Depot in Florida. This was while I was still at Southwest Airlines and before my years as a consultant. The job at Office Depot was a much bigger job, triple the salary, with a tremendous stock plan, and I could live by the beach. To many it would have seemed like a "no-brainer" decision. But for me it was the most difficult decision I ever made. Southwest Airlines was my home, and I felt like I was part of the family. I felt like an owner. I didn't sleep for a month once I was offered the new job. It was a tough decision, but I did eventually accept the opportunity and made the move.

Among other things, I was charged with creating a learning strategy for Office Depot. Just like my challenge at Southwest, people were spread too far and wide for the executives to have a direct impact on all Employees. We also did not have the technology that is available to us today. We couldn't just offer a webinar or e-learning course!

Office Depot had a very different culture, different needs, and different types of people than I had worked with in the past. It was also the fastest growing and most successful retailer in America at the time. Once again I was lost in a world that was unfamiliar to me. On my first day I attended a staff meeting and heard all sorts of terms I had never heard. I didn't know a sku from a ski or a planogram from a planetarium. It was a whole new lingo.

The leaders at Office Depot, just like at Southwest Airlines, wanted to grow a corporation that stood out from all the rest. To me, this meant being willing to take risks and do things differently. I also knew that when you try to do things differently, you have to expect and plan for resistance. One of my most memorable encounters with this principle came when we had an immediate and important training challenge.

Windows 95 was about to be distributed. Microsoft had done an excellent job of creating a buzz around this new software, similar to the more recent release of Apple's iPhone. Office Depot wanted to be well trained and knowledgeable about this software prior to the release date. We had a plan, but then Microsoft moved up the release date. There was no time to implement the training plan we originally outlined. We had about 150 store trainers who traveled all over the world teaching Employees one store at a time. This just wouldn't work given the little time we had left. We wanted to beat the competition to the push and make it appear that Office Depot was the expert in this software.

I went to the chairman of the board with an idea of developing an internal television show to train Employees around the world. It was turned down as a bad idea and waste of money. As I said, doing things differently is often met with resistance. By the time the idea was turned down, there was no time left to implement any other plan. Windows 95 was being released the very next week. I felt that I had no way of pulling this off and making us appear like the experts. I could do nothing and watch the competition's sales soar above ours, or take a big risk and possibly come out on top. I chose the risk.

In less than a week I got Microsoft to agree to pay to set up a television-based training program for all Office Depot Employees to air on the morning of the new release date. I contacted a videographer I knew, found an empty warehouse space, pulled together a team, and worked from five o'clock Friday till early Monday morning. We emptied the warehouse, built a basic sound studio, moved in three satellite trucks, and arranged to have thirty to forty centralized locations where our sales associates could go to watch the training program. Many of these locations were movie theaters that had satellite dishes.

We hired the guy who did the local news to be our anchor and went on air live with Microsoft training Monday morning. Our sales associates could call in questions on the phone and get them answered by Microsoft personnel. It was an early version of today's webinars.

Office Depot outsold every other distribution channel. Our staff, around the globe, was prepared, and we provided exceptional Customer service. It came from thinking differently and providing our Customers with well-trained Employees. Eventually Office Depot TV was on every day and our venders were paying for the airtime. We actually *made* money on our training program.

Jennifer's Take

It is so common for managers to create a new policy every time a new problem crops up. This is reactionary management at its best. The policy is written with the intention of avoiding that problem in the future. Many policies are written because of one or two problem Employees. You end up with a rule book like the one Jeff described as the Big Green Monster. With this practice, the work environment can become so restrictive that no one can breathe without thinking they need to check the policy manual. An effective training program, combined with a values based work environment, is a fantastic method of communicating organizational values. This enables Employees to intuitively know what they should do rather than run to the policy manual every time a decision must be made.

Jeff's story about training at Office Depot is one example of how stepping outside the realm of what you've always done can end up being highly successful for business. Here's a very simple technique you can use in meetings to become more open-minded to new ways of doing things. Typically the initial reaction to a new idea is that someone will quickly bring up why the idea won't work. There are always naysayers who prefer the status quo. Start a new policy. When a new idea is presented, insist that the next five to ten minutes, or more, be spent discussing how this new idea *could* work if you had to make it work. Have fun with it and be creative. Too often you never get to the discussion of how something *could* be done because you never get beyond why it will never work. Being different on the inside will be noticed by Customers on the outside.

When we titled this chapter "Training Instead of Rulebooks" we were not talking only about standard training seminars. Employees receive training through all forms of communication. Use Email, newsletters, and meetings as opportunities to communicate the "right way to do things around here." Actions and decisions, or "walking the talk" is another critical way we teach Employees what's acceptable.

CHAPTER SEVEN

CREATE AN OWNERSHIP ATTITUDE

Jeff's Story

I begin this chapter with one of my favorite stories from my career. It demonstrates a real-life experience of how an Employee ownership program can completely turn around a company. I had the pleasure of spending a week with Jack Stack, the author of an inspiring book called *The Great Game of Business*. Jack was the head of a very large company called Springfield Remanufacturing Corporation. It was the largest employer in Springfield, Missouri. It was a blue-collar workforce, predominately male, and their jobs involved taking all kinds of old parts and machines and making them work like new again.

One morning Jack was reading the *Wall Street Journal*. He happened upon an article about his company. He was shocked to find out, from this article, that his company was being purchased by a much larger company and that his plant would likely be closed. Jack went to work that day and arranged a meeting of all

Employees. He told them that they had two choices: they could do nothing and lose their jobs, or they could buy the business themselves. This group of blue-collar Employees, many of whom were high school dropouts, none of whom had ever owned their own business, came together and purchased the remanufacturing plant. During the purchase process, Jack taught the entire workforce about business economics. He also communicated to them that along with the pride of ownership comes the burden. If the company did well, they'd benefit. If the company didn't do well, they would personally feel that as well. He taught them to read income statements. He taught them about cash flow and balance sheets. They understood, completely. In the end, not only did they keep their jobs and own the company, but they went from a net loss to $2.7 million in profit in just three years.

At Southwest Airlines, we had an Employee stock ownership plan. I never fully understood the value of it until many years into my career. I learned the importance of the ownership attitude both from spending time with Jack Stack and then later in my consulting career when I realized how unusual this ownership attitude really was. I use the term "ownership" broadly. I am in no way suggesting that all ownership plans must include giving shares of the company to Employees. It simply means that Employees experience, in a direct way, the dynamic performance of the company. There are many ways to do this.

The reason behind wanting Employees to act like owners is simple in concept. The owners of the business, or the people in those lead positions, tend to care more and therefore work harder toward the overall success of the company. The success of the business is directly tied to the career and financial success of the owners. This care and concern and connection show in their actions. Successful business owners go over and above the bare minimum of effort. They make decisions as if they are spending their own money (which they are) rather than spending someone else's. They tap into their discretionary effort on a regular basis. Discretionary effort is that level of effort that people can choose to tap into or not. It is the difference between the effort you choose to put into something and the effort you are capable of putting into something. So, wouldn't it be great if we could get Employees to feel and act this same way—like owners? The ability to tap into the discretionary effort of all Employees is a goldmine for any organization. Employee ownership plans force Employees to make decisions as if they were footing the bill themselves. This is the rationale behind Employee ownership.

Here's an example. What if I could convince you that giving Employees an ownership stake in the organization could lead to cost savings and/or revenue enhancements that would generate an additional 8 percent above and beyond what the business needs and is planning on to stay healthy? If we could do this, would an owner be willing to share a portion of the additional profit? Giving Employees some type of ownership stake in the organization does not mean less profit for stakeholders. It means increased profit and success for everyone.

I worked in many organizations where one of my roles was to make Employees more engaged and moti-vated. But my experience has proven that you can only go so far with motivation if you do not somehow, some way, make Employees feel a direct connection between their career and financial success and the success of the business. They must feel it on a daily basis. I'm not downplaying other motivational methods. They are very important. However, I don't know about you, but I can't fake feeling like an owner. I'm either an owner or I'm not. If you want me to consistently act as if I own part of the company, then make me an owner. What I mean by this is to create the people systems needed to ensure that I'm focused on the same goals owners are focused on. Make sure I see the connection between what I do, how satisfied our Customers are, and how well the com-pany performs. Make sure I'm informed. Make sure I'm rewarded for achieving targeted goals.

I worked with many managers who had the opinion that Employees should just be happy to have a job. They should behave like owners because it's expected and because if they don't, they'll be fired. But fear of losing a job will make people act like owners only when neces-sary, only when the boss is watching. They will find out the minimum that they need to do to keep their jobs, and the supervisor may never know the Employee's true potential. The likelihood that Employees will tap into their true potential because of fear, on a consistent basis, is zero.

A recent experience I had as a Customer can illus-trate this point. I was in a large office supply store to purchase software and printer ink. I wasn't sure exactly what I needed, and I sought out the help of one of the Employees. Now, I know that in any business those front-line salespeople are critical. They need to be friendly, fully understand their products, understand what the Customer needs, and make suggestions for other products the Customer might be interested in. None of this occurred on my trip to the store. The salesperson had the attitude that he was annoyed by my questions and I ended up back at home with the wrong products. A few hours later I headed back to the office supply store. This time there was a manager standing with the salesperson with whom I had dealt. The salesperson had a miraculous and sudden change in personality. This time he asked lots of questions. He was friendly and helpful. He made suggestions for another product, which I did end up purchasing. The difference? The manager was watching this time. The Employee felt no personal connection to providing exceptional Customer service or to selling me additional products unless the manager was watching. The only incentive he felt, like many Employees, was that he might lose his job if the manager saw him doing a lousy job. Fear of losing a job will not make Employees act like owners. Instead, Employees will do the minimum they need to keep their jobs. In contrast, people with "ownership" give discretionary effort.

Think about what the typical owner is focused upon. Usually it has something to do with profit margins and Customer service ratings. Now think about the typical performance appraisal form. What does it focus Employees on? Typically there are measures such as coming to work on time, meeting deadlines, and communicating effectively. The more companies I worked within, the more I realized that Employees *must* be focused on and rewarded for the *same* targets as the owners. They should be rewarded for larger accomplishments. One of the great side effects of effectively focusing Employees on these larger goals is that peer pressure kicks in as a supervisory method. When everyone is focused on goals that require team effort to achieve, everyone will suddenly care about what everyone else is doing.

I remember one particular story that illustrates the value of ownership attitudes and peer pressure. I worked as a consultant for a company that had a large unsupervised workforce. The leadership's question to me was "How can we more closely supervise these people—to keep people in line?" My response was not what they expected. They expected methods for closer supervision, or more supervisors, or more rules. My response was to give all Employees, from top to bottom, an ownership stake in the company, and to reduce the number of rules and the number of supervisors. Peer pressure is the most powerful form of supervision, and I explained that they could rely more on this in the changed organization. I asked them questions. *What if everyone feels that they are in the same game together? What if everyone understands simply what we need to do to get to the goal line? What if there were a top-to-bottom profit-sharing plan that would serve to increase productivity, reduce waste, and enhance revenue?*

The leaders of this organization agreed to the plan. We set clear expectations that focused Employees on the big picture. Everyone was trained in basic business finance. We enhanced their communication strategies so that all Employees were regularly informed of how the company was performing, what the competition was doing, and where they were with profit and loss. It was a daily scoreboard that they all grew to understand. With this new environment, Employees became more productive with less supervision, and profits increased. For the Employees, there had never been an incentive to do more than the minimum. Now they all felt personally involved and personally impacted by what each and every Employee contributed. The most effective supervisors are your peers, and when everyone feels like an owner, when everyone has a personal stake in the company, peer pressure to do the right thing begins to take over the need for managers to micromanage. Managers can focus on moving towards goals rather than triage.

Business owners understand business finance. For Employees to act like owners, they also must understand at least the basics of business finance. Never ever underestimate your people's ability to understand and their interest in knowing. As a quick example, both at JetBlue and Southwest Airlines, everyone is required, on their first or second day, to go through a basic airline economics class. Employees are taught about the balance sheet; it's the storybook of the company. Understanding this balance sheet and income statement helps Employees understand their connection to the finances of the company, to the bottom line. With education they understand the game of business, which makes their job a lot more interesting.

At Southwest Airlines, one of the first attempts at educating Employees about airline finances was achieved by having the CFO come to the front of the room with a jar of one hundred pennies. As he described the major expenses for the airline, he took out pennies from the jar. For example, if fuel was 25 percent of total costs for the airline, he'd remove twenty-five pennies from the jar. Once he went through all costs, there were seven pennies left in the jar. This was an eye-opener for most Employees. They could see that there was profit, but they understood how expensive it was to run the airline. They understood that profits were not as large as they had all thought and much harder to achieve than they once believed.

Once Employees understand basic financial information, it is equally important that they be kept informed. Just like owners, Employees must understand how well the company is performing. A once-per-year financial statement is not enough, just as it wouldn't be enough for an owner. This doesn't have to mean completely opening all financial records. It does mean ensuring that Employees understand the target and can see the progress in achieving that target. They won't see the connection between their effort and business performance if no one shows it to them. Great companies design effective scoreboards that all Employees can see. It must be available on a regular basis, like watching the scoreboard at a football game. This scoreboard should include whatever is important to the company. Profits,

Customer service ratings, or progress towards major goals are examples. The entire team should be cheering when the business is performing well. The entire team should be finding what can be done better or differently when the business is not performing well.

Employees who do not understand business finance, or how their actions impact the bottom line, often unknowingly make costly decisions. For example, an aircraft cleaner might not think twice about throwing away that bottle of cleaner that has just an inch left in the bottom. It's almost gone and he'd rather use a full bottle. He doesn't know that this habit practiced by all airline cleaners is costing the company hundreds of thousands of dollars per year. Employees in an office may not think twice about ignoring a call and allowing voice mail to pick up. They're busy talking to their coworker and don't consider that they just lost the opportunity to calm down a frustrated Customer. A project manager might not bring his great idea for a new product to the attention of his supervisor. He's busy enough, and implementing the great idea will just add work to his plate, nothing more. He isn't focused on the fact that if all Employees communicated their new ideas, the business would improve Customer service and significantly increase profit. I could give hundreds of examples. Employees don't get the connection nor is the connection made important to them. An education and communication plan can change this.

When Employees understand the basics of business finance, can see a scoreboard of some kind, and know that their rewards are based on company perfor-mance, they begin to think differently. You can begin to ask them some important questions. *What can we do, above and beyond business as usual, to increase revenue or reduce costs? What can we do to provide an exceptional and memorable Customer experience?* With understand-ing, and with rewards targeted to the right goals, it now becomes important to them to offer their ideas and put in that extra effort to make those ideas happen. They have a vested interest in working towards the same goals, as any business owner would have. You are now tapping the goldmine of discretionary effort. The air-craft cleaner no longer wants to throw away the partial bottle of cleaner. The pilot taxis with one engine to save fuel. The Employees in the office will work hard to take those calls and resolve Customer problems. The project manager will feel a personal stake in finding more pro-ductive methods to accomplish goals. Employees won't tolerate the slackers because it directly impacts their personal compensation.

I worked with many executives who believed that their annual bonus program made Employees feel like owners. The program supposedly gives a bonus based upon individual performance, and bonuses tend to fall within a fairly predicable range. Yet so many of those programs turn into an entitlement program: one that Employees grow to expect and even count on when calculating their annual salary. Because of this, it makes Employees angry if they work hard but get the same bonus, or even a smaller bonus, than they received in the past. These annual bonus programs often fail to identify the right results and provide the much-needed scoreboard. Employees don't understand the direct connection between what they do on a daily basis and the overall successes of the company.

Let me offer an example between the attitude toward a bonus that an owner might have versus the attitude an Employee is likely to have. As an Employee, let's say you received a $1,000 bonus one year. Next year you work even harder but get a $500 bonus. Your attitude? You'd feel cheated. You'd direct your frustration at management. You'd probably think they were just cheap and keeping more profit for themselves.

Now consider the attitude of an owner. An owner understands the profit and loss statement throughout the entire year. The owner sees the ups and downs and how well they are doing. The owner understands the competition and challenges. The $500 bonus makes sense to an owner who understands the "why" behind the bonus. Perhaps the owner knows profits were down because of a new investment that will likely bring huge profits next year. Perhaps the owner understands that profits are down but there are new cost savings or revenue enhancement ideas in the works. Owners feel responsible for bringing improvement. Owners trust that if improvements are made, they will be rewarded. The goal is to make this same connection for Employees.

One criticism I often hear about rewarding Employees for company-wide goals is that it isn't fair to tie individual compensation to factors the Employee can't control. I believe that Employees must be compensated fairly for what they do, and that base pay should be static. I don't believe base pay should be extravagant, just fair. A second part of Employee compensation should be tied to company goals. That is the piece of the compensation program that enables Employees to hit a home run. I think Employees generally understand that, for example, when the economy is in a recession, they shouldn't feel aggrieved when compensation programs produce fair base pay without the home run bonus.

Making Employees feel like owners is one way to help your business make its mark and stand out from the competition. If the incentive you offer Employees to work hard is that they get to keep their jobs, your organization is operating like far too many other mediocre organizations. You are just one of many. Your Employees will feel and act like Employees just as in all other similar organizations. You can only be different if you operate differently on the inside. Employee ownership plans provide all Employees with a laser focus on the important things and with an ownership attitude that cannot be faked. Being an owner is both a burden and a benefit. The burden is that the success of the company now lies partially on the Employee's back. If the business does not succeed, the Employee will feel it more directly. The benefit is both the psychological payback of knowing you're an owner and the ability to see and feel the connection between your efforts and your own bottom line. If you want Employees to act like owners, find some way to *make* them owners.

Jennifer's Take

Employee ownership plans have to do with setting a major and important target, ensuring that all Employees have a laser focus on that target, keeping everyone apprised of where they are in reaching the target, and then rewarding if they make the target. It means greater profits, more focused Employees, and happier Customers. It means tapping into what Jeff referred to as the "goldmine" of discretionary effort.

There are many ways to reward Employees for achieving the same goals that are rewarding for owners. Again, it doesn't mean giving up control and it doesn't have to mean giving away shares of the company. Variable pay programs are one popular method of focusing everyone on company-wide goals. Variable pay is an incentive, based on reaching challenging defined targets, that does not become a part of base pay. It is a onetime payment that focuses everyone on the same goals. Some companies choose to tie variable pay rewards to 401(k) contributions and company stock options as well. Rewards such as these do not impact fixed costs, and change from year to year based upon targeted goals and achievement of those goals.

With traditional merit increases, Employees tend to get rewarded for business as usual. Also, they retain that salary increase regardless of future performance of the company. The reward increases annual fixed costs. Merit increases have the effect of rewarding Employees, year after year, more for staying with the company than for actual individual performance levels. While Employee retention is very important, it should not be the sole focus of the compensation reward plan. At some point in the game, the number of years of experience a person has no longer automatically means he or she is more productive and valuable. The important aspect here is that everyone fully understands the connection between their role in the company, their individual performance, and overall company achievements.

All Employees, anywhere they are, have the choice between doing the bare minimum or tapping into their discretionary effort. People do this in jobs, any task or goal they work toward, and even in relationships. A boss could stay an hour late to talk to an Employee, or just go home. An Employee could go help a Customer, or pretend he doesn't notice help is needed. Discretionary effort is a valued commodity, an extraordinarily competitive issue; and at work, the environment will determine whether and how often Employees will tap into that effort. Creating the systems so that Employees truly have an ownership stake is a surefire way to tap into everyone's full potential. Exceptional Customer service comes from this type of exceptional effort.

In this chapter, there is a brief mention of the typical rating factors on performance appraisal forms and how these are often so different than the specific targets owners are focused upon. I want to focus on this point in a little more detail because it's a fairly simple change managers can make to their performance appraisal forms. Jeff mentions that typical performance appraisal measures include things like coming to work on time, meeting deadlines, and communicating effectively. If Employees do these things well, they receive a 5 percent salary increase. This scenario, which is typical in most organizations, leaves Employees focusing on individual tasks and expectations and *not* on the actual measures of company success.

An owner will understand the connection between those typical individual performance measures and company success. The owner knows that if everyone does these certain things well, the company will reap the rewards. An owner wants to meet deadlines *not* so that she will get an outstanding performance appraisal and perhaps get a 5 percent raise, but because she wants to provide outstanding Customer service, beat competition into new territories, and increase profits. An owner thinks bigger because she is rewarded for these bigger successes.

Performance management practices can go a long way in focusing Employees on the same things that owners, or those in leadership positions, must focus on. When designing that performance appraisal form, compensation plan, or reward program, add in measures for departmental and companywide achievements. Individual performance measures don't have to be completely deleted, but if Employees don't directly see the connection between company success and their rewards then they will never have that ownership dedication and focus. Employees must also be able to regularly see some type of scoreboard to see progress towards these goals. Providing incentives towards those larger, more meaningful goals, and providing a scoreboard, helps Employees understand the *why* behind individual performance measures. It provides purpose. It improves motivation.

Even in nonprofit organizations, reward systems can focus on the bigger picture, giving Employees the feel of ownership. For a nonprofit, typical "big picture" goals will include increasing membership or clients or students. Goals may include decreasing wasteful costs and finding ways to increase revenue. A private school may be looking at how to increase student retention. Incentives can be tied to these organization-wide goals. Regular communication from leadership can serve as the scoreboard. You can reward people in many ways such as increasing benefits, training, 401(k) contributions, or bonuses when costs are reduced and revenue is enhanced even at a nonprofit. The key is to make sure Employees see and feel the connection between having everyone come together with their "discretionary effort" and the end result and rewards for doing so.

Focused and motivated Employees will always provide a better experience for Customers than those who are just there to earn a paycheck. If you want Employees to consistently tap into discretionary effort, make sure they're focused on the same goals owners are focused on. Make sure they see the connection between what they do and how well the company performs. Make sure they're informed. And make sure they're rewarded when those targeted goals are reached.

CHAPTER EIGHT

INSIDE OUT CUSTOMER SERVICE

Jeff's Story

If you want to stand out from the competition and provide exceptional Customer service, you have to be willing to take risks and do things differently. You won't develop a reputation for doing things differently if all of your people practices on the inside of the company are exactly like the standard practices at other companies. You have to be different on the inside to be different on the outside.

To better understand the concept of "Inside Out Customer Service," it helps to think at the individual level. Consider a person who is kind, honest, and caring. If he truly has all of these characteristics, people around him will know that. He'll be known as a trustworthy and caring person. Now consider someone who is a liar, a thief, and self-centered. He might be able to hide these characteristics well to some, for a period of time, but eventually people will figure him out. What you are on the inside becomes apparent on the outside. The same is true for organizations.

Since the game of business involves standing out from the competition, it's important to do things differently on the inside of your organization. One of my clients as a consultant was a large gaming company based in Las Vegas. I was always amazed by the people who would spend hours and hours at the slot machines, somehow imagining that they'd beat the odds without doing anything different from all the gamblers who'd lost it all. They'd look at all of the mega resorts on the Vegas strip, the ones that cost billions of dollars, and yet still think that they were going to come out ahead of the game without doing anything different from the people whose losses built the swanky properties. Too many businesses do the same thing—they just pull the lever like everyone else and hope that luck brings success. It doesn't work that way.

I do realize that certain professional gamblers seem to have something figured out that I haven't, and a few of those end up doing quite well. For instance, the winners of the World Series of Poker *must* have found some patterns of behavior that for them work well as they strive to win each hand. I, on the other hand, am clueless as to what these patterns are. I see many poker players wearing sunglasses or carrying lucky charms, while attempting to show little to no emotion, but that's about the extent of my understanding. Somehow I don't think the sunglasses or lucky charm would help me that much in business.

In the business world, if you're going to be the 1 percent that shines above the rest, the winner, you too have to do something different. If all you do is roll the dice and hope for the best, the odds will always be against you. If you run your business just like everyone else runs their business, you're going to be *just like* everyone else. You're leaving your career and the success of your business to the luck of the draw. If you want to be different, you have to *do* something different.

As a consultant I would dive in and actually work as an Employee within the organization. There was a time when I was the temporary human resources director of five major companies at one time. Because of this, I have had the opportunity to go through far more new Employee orientations than the average person. The importance of organizations being the same on the inside as they expect to be viewed on the outside was reaffirmed with each and every new Employee orientation I went through.

Here's why. I realized early on that too often there are two completely different new Employee orientations when starting a job. There is the formal orientation that includes a review of your job description, a tour of the building, an explanation of payroll schedule and benefits package, and possibly an introduction to some of your colleagues. This orientation actually begins in the interview process when they are trying to convince you to come to work for them. The sales pitch.

The second and most authentic orientation begins once that first "canned" orientation is over. You're now hired. You've been through the corporate required orientation, and now you're left alone at your desk or workstation. "WHAM!" the real orientation now hits you like a ton of bricks. This one occurs quickly with peers and observations. You find out what it's really like to work here. You find out what everyone thinks of the boss. Most importantly, you find an answer to the question "What is the minimum I need to do to keep my job?" You might be willing to do more, but you definitely figure out that minimum by watching the people around you. Expectations and normal standards of behavior become far more clear and real than what you may have read in the Employee handbook.

The best companies I worked with throughout my career had little difference between the formal orientation and the real orientation. What I was told about the company matched the expectations I felt once inside of the company. Similarly, what Customers see, feel, and experience from the company is exactly what its Employees see, feel, and experience on the inside of the company. It's just like values; there should be *one* set of values and *one* orientation.

If Employees are happy, Customers are happy. If you are creative and innovative in how you manage your company, Customers will see creativity and innovation in your products and services. If you look worn down on the inside, you probably look worn down on the outside, just like the old green van.

The subject of doing something different, inside and out, was a major topic of conversation during those initial meetings I mentioned when JetBlue was created. In these initial meetings it seemed that all of their plans were fairly predictable, standard plans you'd expect as you begin creating a new airline. The problem was that they wanted to be different, yet, at least initially, none of the ideas seemed different.

Very experienced people sometimes look at things with too many limitations: "can't do that," "this won't work," "already tried that," etc. The path of least resistance is to create what you already know. However, there wasn't need for another United or Delta or American. There were plenty of those airlines, and they were flying with empty seats. If we wanted to be different, we had to put something different into the building blocks of this new airline. You are on the outside what you are on the inside.

We began a discussion of what the Customer experience was going to be like with this new airline. I facilitated an activity with everyone involved at the time to begin the brainstorming process of doing things differently. They had to find the reasons why people would want to fly this new airline instead of all the existing choices. The activity involved thinking like a Customer, but for a business that none of these airline executives had ever actually owned or worked in. We chose a cab company. By choosing a company none of them had ever worked within, they would think only like a Customer.

They were asked to come up with a list of all the basic necessities for starting a cab company. What would they need before they could ever open their doors? They listed things like cars, insurance, radios, and drivers. When they couldn't think of anything else, they were asked to add to the list by thinking about what they could offer their

Customers that added value to the experience and was different from other cab companies. What would distinguish them from the competitor? They came up with ideas such as a frequent taxicab program and a guaranteed on-time program.

When they had exhausted all of their ideas again, they were asked to come up with a final list that included outrageously different ways this cab company could service their Customers. There were no rules; they could come up with any idea. What would a dream cab ride look like to the Customer? They came up with ideas such as having a massage while in the cab, and having a backseat bar available for riders.

When their list was done, we spent a few minutes crossing off the items that absolutely could never be done. We were left with many ideas that would definitely make this cab company stand out from all the rest! We then categorized each idea into a quadrant with two scales as in Figure 3: highly valuable to the Customer, and doable. The ideas in the top right quadrant, highly valuable and doable, would then get further analysis.

Figure 3: Categorizing New Ideas: Doable and Valuable

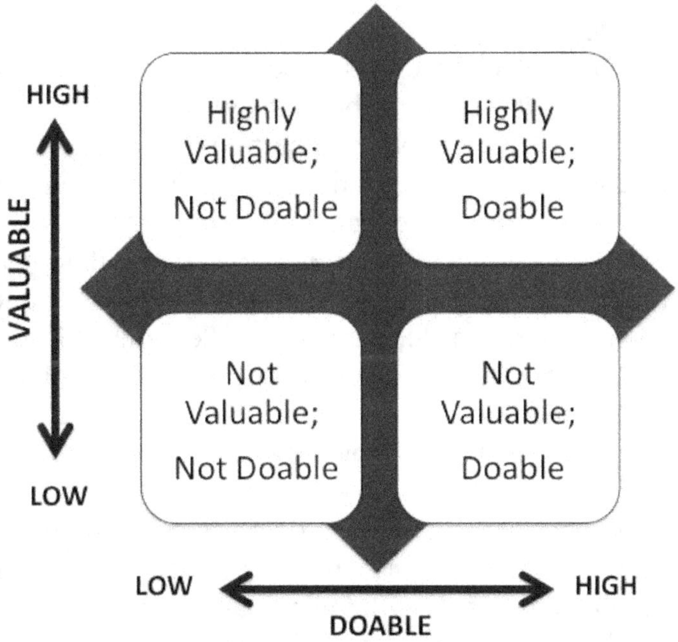

This highly experienced group of executives repre-senting most of the major airlines existing at the time began to think differently. Rather than thinking like an experienced airline executive, they began thinking like Customers. Brainstorming and creativity were needed more than the logical and rational steps to building another airline like all the rest. *What do Customers want? What would make this new airline unique? How could they create a new Customer base from people who generally chose other modes of transportation or who chose not to travel at all?*

I used this activity with many clients during my consulting career. It's a fun exercise for any business, and the purpose is to learn how to think about new and different ideas to help your business stand out from the rest. As I used this activity with multiple clients, I noticed an interesting pattern. Although some great ideas came out of the activity, it was rare for anyone to bring up ideas about hiring differently or rewarding, communicating, or motivating differently. I would often have to provide those initial ideas to get everyone thinking along these lines. Remember, if you want to be different to your Customers, have unique policies and practices on the inside with Employees as well. This alone will make your company stand out from the rest.

One specific example of doing things differently at JetBlue had to do with their call centers. All airlines have call centers. They handle large volumes of calls and deal with Customer service issues, reservations, changes in reservations, etc. JetBlue wanted to open their call center in Salt Lake City. There were already twelve other major call centers in this city. The city was known for having a great work ethic, the weather was good, and it had a fairly low cost of living. But with so many call centers already in that city, the JetBlue executives ran the risk of having trouble recruiting and retaining quality Employees. If the call center next door just offered twenty cents more per hour, Employees would leave and go next door. The jobs were exactly the same. JetBlue had to do something differently while still holding down costs.

The decision was made to put call center Employees in their homes. The goal was to be a low-cost airline, and this saved the airline about 30 percent above the normal costs of building and operating a call center. Furthermore, Employees were thrilled with the opportunity to be able to work from home without the cost of commuting, uniforms, dry cleaning, childcare, etc. This was at a time when telecommuting was not even on people's radar. It was a new concept, and we were flooded with job applications. These excited Employees provided great Customer care. As discussed in a previous chapter, doing something to increase your qualified applicant pool has a profound impact on your ability to hire great Employees. JetBlue did something different for their Employees, and it had a major impact on the Customer service experience they provided and on their organizational culture.

An example of how Southwest Airlines was different could be seen by watching one of their famous "ten-minute turnarounds." I mentioned this in an earlier chapter when talking about executives who worked in line positions. The policy back then was to have a plane come into the gate and head back out of the gate with new passengers in just ten minutes. Our people took this seriously. They would practically attack the plane when it came into the gate. It was like watching an Indy pit crew for a Boeing 737. It was also nothing like how the other airlines handled it. I'd watch Employees of other airlines loiter through their much longer turnarounds, and they all looked somehow depressed compared to our people. At Southwest Airlines, everyone hustled. It wasn't our compensation program because we paid less than every other major airline. We were different, and it was clearly evident. There was an ownership attitude at Southwest Airlines. We were on the inside what Customers felt on the outside.

Previously I mentioned that there are hundreds of different touch points, or methods to influence Employees. There are also hundreds of different touch points that can detract or add value for your Customers. At each of these touch points, there is the potential to do something memorable, something different, for your Customer. You begin by thinking differently and then doing things differently than the competition.

Here is the long and short of it—I have looked at this thing for years—up, down, sideways, one industry to another, one country to another, and here is what I learned. Don't ever expect the experience of your Customer to be anything different than the experience you provide for your Employee internally—it won't work! Be exactly what you are on the inside as you want to be on the outside. You want indifferent service to your Customers? No problem—you can treat your people as disposable on the inside. You want flexible, humorous, discretionary effort to be seen by Customers externally? Better figure out how to mirror that inside—exactly.

Jennifer's Take

I've found that most leaders want their company to be viewed as "superior" to the competition, yet so much of what goes on in the inside of the company is exactly the same as what goes on in the inside of the competition's company. That is, the same types of meetings, policies, procedures, hiring practices, rewards programs, organizational charts, etc., are evident in almost every business, including those that want to stand out from the crowd in big ways. If you want to exhibit something different and better to your Customers than the competition, you must do something better and different on the inside of the company. The truth is…inside to Employees looks just like outside to Customers.

When Customer service ratings are down, a natural reaction is to send front-line Employees to a Customer service–training program. While this natural reaction may play a part in resolving the real problem, it is a piecemeal approach that ignores the full connection between the work environment and the Customer experience. It is all too common to focus only on what we can do externally to be better and different from other businesses.

Because the importance of doing things differently on the inside is so often overlooked, it is now common practice to simply download a ready-to-use Employee handbook, approved by attorneys. The fear of a lawsuit makes people forget about the importance of having a unique brand beginning with internal policies and procedures. Don't get me wrong. Having a legally sound Employee manual is a must. However, also remember the personality of the company you're developing. Remember how you want Employees to feel when they read the handbook. Pages and pages of nothing but rigid rules are not memorable nor motivating.

Jeff's stories in this chapter reminded me over and over again of the importance of providing a realistic preview of the job to all applicants. So often we want to paint this wonderful picture of the workplace to get a "yes" from our favorite job candidate. But you're doing yourself and the applicant a disservice. If there are challenges, imperfections, and struggles within your company, be honest about it. Why? Because you want an Employee who can handle what's real on the inside and perhaps know how to make it better. You want someone who is excited for the challenge.

SUMMARY

BE GENUINE—BE AUTHENTIC

The "Inside Out" ideas we've presented in this book all point to one major lesson. That is, be genuine. It will get you noticed! To determine where your business falls on the genuineness scale, ask yourself the following questions:

- ❖ If satisfied Customers were to come work within your business, would they still have the same positive opinions they have as Customers? Would their impressions of your business change?
- ❖ Do you have two separate new-Employee orientations? Do new hires have one impression of the job but a whole new impression after a few weeks of working there?
- ❖ Would your Employees agree that they are treated by management exactly how they are expected to treat Customers?

We have seen plenty of businesses survive despite the fact that they do not meet this particular measurement of genuineness. There is chaos and conflict and disengagement on the inside, but management does their best to portray a much different image on the outside. They may survive, but they do not thrive. The decision is whether you want to simply stay afloat or whether you want to build a satisfied and loyal Customer base, develop a great reputation as a company, and make your competition irrelevant. If these goals are more in line with where you want to be, you must create on the inside what you want to be known for on the outside.

Most of us have, at one time or another, read a book or attended a seminar and walked away filled with ideas for improvement. But the daily grind sets back in, old habits die hard, and after a few weeks you can hardly remember those great ideas. Change is more likely if you can break down complex ideas into something more logical and simple. For this reason, we've summarized this book with ten logical and simple concepts we hope you'll continue to consider, even after the next few weeks go by.

Number One: Great Organizations Are Built Around a Strategic Set of Values

Values underlie all behavior and decisions whether we're talking about individuals or organizations. Take a look all the way back to the U.S. Constitution, which clearly outlines values and has stood the test of time despite how much the world has changed. Leaders can strategically define values and integrate them into all people practices, or roll the dice and allow any values to grow.

Number Two: MMFI: Make Me Feel Important

This is the very essence of motivation. The more ways that you validate who and what people are, the more chance you will get an emotional connection with them. This connection provides purpose and taps into Employees' desire to do the very best job they can do. If they don't feel important, they won't do their best.

Number Three: Hire and Fire for Attitude

We'll take a chance on an enthusiastic individual any day. You can't train people to be nice! Attitude can make or break a career.

Number Four: Take Risks and Be Different

Doing things the same old way is too easy. Doing something better and different brings risks. But it also brings opportunity, learning experiences, and new insight.

Number Five: Don't Overlook Training

When budgets are tight, training is often the first investment to go. Yet a lack of training is what is truly expensive to organizations. Not providing training on how to hire well doesn't save money; it costs money. Turnover and performance problems are expensive. It doesn't save money to micromanage your Employees because they can't make decisions on their own. If your training program is not providing a huge return on investment, it needs to be redesigned, not eliminated.

Number Six: Define the "Right Way" through Your Values System

Clearly defined values enable you to define the behaviors expected from all Employees. Too many organizations focus only on achieving the right results. To grow your ideal culture, to stand out from the competition, all Employees must understand "how things should be done around here." Do you collaborate or backstab your way to a goal? Do you innovate or stick with established procedures? Values help determine the "right way."

Number Seven: You Cannot Impose Culture; You Can Only Create Environment

Organizational culture is made up of the values and beliefs that underlie all behaviors and decisions when the boss isn't watching. You cannot describe an ideal culture and then impose it from the top down. Instead, focus on the elements of your work environment and develop each of those with organizational values acting as the guide and ideal culture as the goal. The success of an organization comes down to the work environment that is created.

Number Eight: Experience Your Decisions

If you're in a management or leadership position, it is all too easy to dictate new policies and rules without having a clear understanding of the domino effect of those decisions. Take the time to talk to Employees at all levels of the organization. You don't have a monopoly on good ideas. Take time to work in positions at every level. Nothing will give you better insight than firsthand experience.

Number Nine: Little Things Mean a Lot

When you think about ways to motivate Employees, it's natural to immediately think about rewards. Yet my determination of whether I'm having a good day versus a bad day has much more to do with the little things. Did I get a "thank you" from the boss? Did my colleague notice I needed help? Did I get to take my lunch break today? Was my boss in a good mood? Little things mean a lot, and Customers will feel the impact of those little things that are impacting your Employees' day.

Number Ten: Exceptional Organizations Consistently Tap the Discretionary Effort of Their People

We all have a level of effort we are capable of giving. We also know exactly the level of effort we need to give in order to just get by. Your organization may survive even if you don't follow the principles in this book. Yet you will be operating with everyone's "just getting by" level of effort. Just think of what could be accomplished if we all worked up to our true capabilities. Discretionary effort is available in any organization but often is a goldmine yet to be discovered. When you create a great work environment, you'll tap into that discretionary effort, and your Customers will notice the difference.

In summary, the place to start in improving Customer service is inside the organization. If Employees are treated with disdain, don't expect Customers to be treated with respect. If Employees experience conflict in the work environment, Customers will experience that conflict. Build a work environment that treats Employees exactly how Customers should be treated. Successful organizations are genuine.

EPILOGUE

Shortly after completing this book, Jeff Sullivan, my brother, passed away. I'm thankful that I was able to capture many of his stories and business lessons. I hope you enjoyed them too. The book was intended to be the first in a series of five short books. Perhaps I'll work towards that in his honor.

Jeff had much to offer the world. He was creative, kind, fun, and had a heart for helping people achieve great things. He had the best laugh ever! All who had the privilege of knowing him miss him greatly.

Jennifer Good